If you've always preferred small crochet projects, you're going to love the easy afghans in this decorator collection. Each starts out as single blocks or strips. Medium weight yarn makes them soft and cozy.

LEISURE ARTS, INC. • Maumelle, Arkansas

Airy Squares

●●○○ **EASY**

Finished Size: 50" x 62" (127 cm x 157.5 cm)

SHOPPING LIST

Yarn (Medium Weight)
[3.5 ounces, 175 yards
(100 grams, 160 meters) per skein]:
☐ MC (Red) - 9 skeins
☐ CC (Brown) - 5 skeins

Crochet Hook
☐ Size I (5.5 mm)
   or size needed for gauge

Additional Supplies
☐ Yarn needle

GAUGE INFORMATION
One Square = 6" (15.25 cm)
Gauge Swatch: 4" (10 cm) diameter
Work same as Solid Square, page 4,
through Rnd 3: 48 sc and 16 sps.

STITCH GUIDE
TREBLE CROCHET *(abbreviated tr)*
YO twice, insert hook in sp indicated, YO and pull up a loop (4 loops on hook), (YO and draw through 2 loops on hook) 3 times.

2-DC CLUSTER (uses one sp)
★ YO, insert hook in sp indicated, YO and pull up a loop, YO and draw through 2 loops on hook; repeat from ★ once **more**, YO and draw through all 3 loops on hook.

3-DC CLUSTER (uses one sp)
★ YO, insert hook in sp indicated, YO and pull up a loop, YO and draw through 2 loops on hook; repeat from ★ 2 times **more**, YO and draw through all 4 loops on hook.

DECREASE (uses next 3 ch-1 sps)
YO, † insert hook in **next** ch-1 sp, YO and pull up a loop, YO and draw through 2 loops on hook †, YO skip **next** ch-1 sp, repeat from † to † once, YO and draw through all 3 loops on hook (**counts as one dc**).

SOLID SQUARE (Make 40)

With MC, ch 5; join with slip st to form a ring.

Rnd 1 (Right side)**:** Ch 4 (**counts as first dc plus ch 1, now and throughout**), (dc in ring, ch 1) 7 times; join with slip st to first dc: 8 dc and 8 ch-1 sps.

Note: Loop a short piece of yarn around any stitch to mark Rnd 1 as **right** side.

Rnd 2: (Slip st, ch 2, work 2-dc Cluster) in next ch-1 sp, (ch 3, work 3-dc Cluster in next ch-1 sp) around, ch 1, hdc in top of first 2-dc Cluster to form last ch-3 sp.

Rnd 3: Ch 1, (sc, ch 3, 3 sc) in last ch-3 sp made, ch 1, ★ (3 sc, ch 3, 3 sc) in next ch-3 sp, ch 1; repeat from ★ around, 2 sc in same sp as first sc; join with slip st to first sc: 48 sc and 16 sps.

Rnd 4: Slip st in next ch-3 sp, ch 4, (dc in same sp, ch 1) twice, skip next ch-1 sp, ★ (dc, ch 1) 4 times in next ch-3 sp, skip next ch-1 sp; repeat from ★ around, dc in same sp as first slip st, ch 1; join with slip st to first dc: 32 dc and 32 ch-1 sps.

Rnd 5: Slip st in next ch-1 sp, ch 9 (**counts as first tr plus ch 5**), tr in same sp, ★ † ch 3, decrease, ch 3, sc in next ch-1 sp, ch 3, decrease, ch 3 †, (tr, ch 5, tr) in next ch-1 sp; repeat from ★ 2 times **more**, then repeat from † to † once; join with slip st to first tr: 20 sts and 20 sps.

Rnd 6: (Slip st, ch 1, 6 sc) in next corner ch-5 sp, sc in next tr, (3 sc in next ch-3 sp, sc in next st) 4 times, ★ 6 sc in next corner ch-5 sp, sc in next tr, (3 sc in next ch-3 sp, sc in next st) 4 times; repeat from ★ 2 times **more**; join with slip st to first sc, finish off: 92 sc.

TWO-TONE SQUARE (Make 40)

With CC, ch 5; join with slip st to form a ring.

Rnd 1 (Right side)**:** Ch 4, (dc in ring, ch 1) 7 times; join with slip st to first dc, finish off: 8 dc and 8 ch-1 sps.

Note: Mark Rnd 1 as **right** side.

Rnd 2: With **right** side facing, join MC with slip st in any ch-1 sp; ch 2, work 2-dc Cluster in same sp, ch 3, (work 3-dc Cluster in next ch-1 sp, ch 3) around; join with slip st to top of first 2-dc Cluster, finish off.

Rnd 3: With **right** side facing, join CC with sc in any ch-3 sp *(see Joining With Sc, page 30)*; (2 sc, ch 3, 3 sc) in same sp, ch 1, ★ (3 sc, ch 3, 3 sc) in next ch-3 sp, ch 1; repeat from ★ around; join with slip st to first sc, finish off: 48 sc and 16 sps.

Rnd 4: With **right** side facing, join MC with dc in any ch-3 sp *(see Joining With Dc, page 30)*; ch 1, (dc in same sp, ch 1) 3 times, skip next ch-1 sp, ★ (dc, ch 1) 4 times in next ch-3 sp, skip next ch-1 sp; repeat from ★ around; join with slip st to first dc, finish off: 32 dc and 32 ch-1 sps.

Rnd 5: With **right** side facing, skip first ch-1 sp after joining and join CC with slip st in next ch-1 sp; ch 9, tr in same sp, ★ † ch 3, decrease, ch 3, sc in next ch-1 sp, ch 3, decrease, ch 3 †, (tr, ch 5, tr) in next ch-1 sp; repeat from ★ 2 times **more**, then repeat from † to † once; join with slip st to first tr, do **not** finish off: 20 sts and 20 sps.

Rnd 6: (Slip st, ch 1, 6 sc) in next corner ch-5 sp, sc in next tr, (3 sc in next ch-3 sp, sc in next st) 4 times, ★ 6 sc in next corner ch-5 sp, sc in next tr, (3 sc in next ch-3 sp, sc in next st) 4 times; repeat from ★ 2 times **more**; join with slip st to first sc, finish off: 92 sc.

ASSEMBLY

A matching color of smooth yarn may be used if your yarn tends to break easily.

With **wrong** sides together, using Placement Diagram as a guide and working through **inside** loops on **both** pieces, whipstitch Squares together with MC *(Fig. 5c, page 31)*, forming 8 vertical strips of 10 Squares each, beginning in fourth sc of first corner and ending in third sc of next corner; then whipstitch strips together in same manner.

EDGING

Rnd 1: With **right** side facing, join MC with sc in fourth sc of any corner; ★ sc in each sc across ending in third sc of next corner, ch 1; repeat from ★ around; join with slip st to first sc.

Rnd 2: Ch 1, sc in same st as joining and in each sc around working one sc in each corner ch-1 sp; join with slip st to first sc.

Rnd 3: Ch 1, sc in same st as joining and in each sc around working 3 sc in each corner sc; join with slip st to first sc, finish off.

Design by Melissa Leapman.

PLACEMENT DIAGRAM

KEY

Solid Squares

Two-Tone Squares

Simply Pretty

●●○○ **EASY**

Finished Size: 48" x 67" (122 cm x 170 cm)

SHOPPING LIST

Yarn (Medium Weight)

[3.5 ounces, 175 yards

(100 grams, 160 meters) per skein]:

☐ MC (Grey) - 9 skeins

☐ Color A (Pink) - 4 skeins

☐ Color B (Lt Grey) - 4 skeins

Crochet Hook

☐ Size H (5 mm)

 or size needed for gauge

Additional Supplies

☐ Yarn needle

GAUGE INFORMATION

One Square = 8" (20.5 cm)

Gauge Swatch: 5" (12.75 cm)

Work same as Square thru Rnd 5: 68 dc and 4 corner ch-3 sps.

STITCH GUIDE

TREBLE CROCHET *(abbreviated tr)*

YO twice, insert hook in st or sp indicated, YO and pull up a loop (4 loops on hook), (YO and draw through 2 loops on hook) 3 times.

SQUARE (Make 48)

With Color B, ch 5; join with slip st to form a ring.

Rnd 1: Ch 1, (3 sc, ch 2) 4 times in ring; join with slip st to first sc: 12 sc and 4 ch-2 sps.

Rnd 2 (Right side)**:** Ch 3 (**counts as first dc**), turn; (2 dc, ch 3, 2 dc) in next corner ch-2 sp, dc in next sc, skip next sc, ★ dc in next sc, (2 dc, ch 3, 2 dc) in next corner ch-2 sp, dc in next sc, skip next sc; repeat from ★ 2 times **more**; join with slip st to first dc, finish off: 24 dc and 4 corner ch-3 sps.

Note: Loop a short piece of yarn around any stitch to mark Rnd 2 as **right** side.

Rnd 3: With **right** side facing, join Color A with dc in any corner ch-3 sp *(see Joining With Dc, page 30)*; (dc, ch 3, 2 dc) in same sp, skip next 3 dc, (tr, ch 3, tr) in sp **before** next dc *(Fig. 4, page 31)*, ★ (2 dc, ch 3, 2 dc) in next corner ch-3 sp, skip next 3 dc, (tr, ch 3, tr) in sp **before** next dc; repeat from ★ 2 times **more**; join with slip st to first dc, finish off: 24 sts and 8 ch-3 sps.

Rnd 4: With **right** side facing, join MC with dc in any corner ch-3 sp; (dc, ch 3, 2 dc) in same sp, dc in next 3 sts, 3 dc in next ch-3 sp, dc in next 3 sts, ★ (2 dc, ch 3, 2 dc) in next corner ch-3 sp, dc in next 3 sts, 3 dc in next ch-3 sp, dc in next 3 sts; repeat from ★ 2 times **more**; join with slip st to first dc, finish off: 52 dc and 4 corner ch-3 sps.

Rnd 5: With **right** side facing, join Color B with dc in any corner ch-3 sp; (dc, ch 3, 2 dc) in same sp, ★ † dc in next 2 dc, skip next dc, 3 dc in next dc, (skip next 2 dc, 3 dc in next dc) twice, skip next dc, dc in next 2 dc †, (2 dc, ch 3, 2 dc) in next corner ch-3 sp; repeat from ★ 2 times **more**, then repeat from † to † once; join with slip st to first dc, finish off: 68 dc and 4 corner ch-3 sps.

Rnd 6: With **right** side facing, join Color A with dc in any corner ch-3 sp; (dc, ch 3, 2 dc) in same sp, ★ † skip next 3 dc, (tr, ch 3, tr) in next dc, [skip next 4 dc, (tr, ch 3, tr) in next dc] twice †, (2 dc, ch 3, 2 dc) in next corner ch-3 sp; repeat from ★ 2 times **more**, then repeat from † to † once; join with slip st to first dc, finish off: 40 sts and 16 ch-3 sps.

Rnd 7: With **right** side facing, join MC with dc in any corner ch-3 sp; dc in same sp, ★ † dc in next 3 sts, 3 dc in next ch-3 sp, (dc in next 2 tr, 3 dc in next ch-3 sp) twice, dc in next 3 sts †, (2 dc, ch 3, 2 dc) in next corner ch-3 sp; repeat from ★ 2 times **more**, then repeat from † to † once, 2 dc in same corner sp as first dc, ch 1, hdc in first dc to form last corner ch-3 sp, do **not** finish off: 92 dc and 4 corner ch-3 sps.

Rnd 8: Ch 3, dc in last corner ch-3 sp made, ★ † dc in next dc and in each dc across to next corner ch-3 sp †, (2 dc, ch 3, 2 dc) in corner sp; repeat from ★ 2 times **more**, then repeat from † to † once, 2 dc in same corner sp as first dc, ch 1, hdc in first dc to form last corner ch-3 sp, finish off: 108 dc and 4 corner ch-3 sps.

ASSEMBLY

A matching color of smooth yarn may be used if your yarn tends to break easily.

With **wrong** sides together and working through **inside** loops on **both** pieces, whipstitch Squares together with MC *(Fig. 5c, page 31)*, forming 6 vertical strips of 8 Squares each, beginning and ending in center ch of each corner; then whipstitch strips together in same manner.

EDGING

Row 1: With **right** side facing and working across short edge, join Color A with dc in first corner ch-3 sp; dc in same sp, dc in next 27 dc, (dc in sp on **same** Square and in sp on **next** Square, dc in next 27 dc) across to next corner ch-3 sp, 2 dc in corner sp: 176 dc.

Row 2: Ch 3, **turn**; dc in next dc and in each dc across; finish off.

Row 3: With **right** side facing, join Color B with dc in first dc; dc in next dc and in each dc across; finish off.

Row 4: With **wrong** side facing, join MC with sc in first dc; sc in each dc across; finish off.

Repeat across opposite short edge.

Design by Mary Lamb Becker.

All-Around Favorite

 ●●○○ **EASY**

Finished Size: 47½" x 61" (120.5 cm x 155 cm)

SHOPPING LIST

Yarn (Medium Weight)

[3.5 ounces, 208 yards
(100 grams, 190 meters) per skein]:
- ☐ MC (White) - 6 skeins
- ☐ Color A (Dk Blue) - 2 skeins
- ☐ Color B (Blue) - 2 skeins
- ☐ Color C (Lt Blue) - 1 skein

Crochet Hook
- ☐ Size I (5.5 mm)
  or size needed for gauge

Additional Supplies
- ☐ Yarn needle

GAUGE INFORMATION

One Square = 6¾" (17.25 cm)
Gauge Swatch:
   4½" (11.5 cm) diameter
Work same as Square thru Rnd 4:
48 dc.

STITCH GUIDE

TREBLE CROCHET *(abbreviated tr)*
YO twice, insert hook in st indicated, YO and pull up a loop (4 loops on hook), (YO and draw through 2 loops on hook) 3 times.

PUFF ST *(uses one st or sp)*
★ YO, insert hook in st or sp indicated, YO and pull up a loop even with loop on hook; repeat from ★ once **more**, YO and draw through all 5 loops on hook.

SQUARE (Make 48 **total**)

Make the following number of squares using the color indicated for Rnds 1, 2, and 6: 24 with Color B and 12 **each** with Color A and Color C.

With color indicated, ch 5; join with slip st to form a ring.

Rnd 1 (Right side): Ch 4 (**counts as first dc plus ch 1, now and throughout**), (dc in ring, ch 1) 9 times; join with slip st to first dc: 10 dc.

Note: Loop a short piece of yarn around any stitch to mark Rnd 1 as **right** side.

Rnd 2: Ch 1, work Puff St in same st as joining, ch 3, (work Puff St in next dc, ch 3) around; join with slip st to top of first Puff St, finish off: 10 Puff Sts and 10 ch-3 sps.

Rnd 3: With **right** side facing, join MC with sc in any ch-3 sp *(see Joining With Sc, page 30)*; 3 sc in same sp, 4 sc in next ch-3 sp and in each ch-3 sp around; join with slip st to first sc: 40 sc.

Rnd 4: Ch 3 (**counts as first dc, now and throughout**), dc in same st as joining and in next 4 sc, (2 dc in next sc, dc in next 4 sc) around; join with slip st to first dc: 48 dc.

Rnd 5: Ch 4, (tr, ch 3, tr, ch 1, dc) in same st as joining, ★ † ch 1, skip next dc, dc in next dc, ch 1, skip next dc, hdc in next dc, ch 1, skip next dc, sc in next dc, ch 1, skip next dc, hdc in next dc, ch 1, skip next dc, dc in next dc, ch 1, skip next dc †, (dc, ch 1, tr, ch 3, tr, ch 1, dc) in next dc; repeat from ★ 2 times **more**, then repeat from † to † once; join with slip st to first dc, finish off: 36 sts and 36 sps.

Rnd 6: With **right** side facing, join color indicated with slip st in any corner ch-3 sp; ch 1, work (Puff St, ch 3, Puff St) in same sp, ch 2, ★ (work Puff St in next ch-1 sp, ch 2) across to next corner ch-3 sp, work (Puff St, ch 3, Puff St) in corner sp, ch 2; repeat from ★ 2 times **more**, (work Puff St in next ch-1 sp, ch 2) across; join with slip st to top of first Puff St, finish off: 40 Puff Sts and 40 sps.

Rnd 7: With **right** side facing, join MC with hdc in any corner ch-3 sp *(see Joining With Hdc, page 30)*; ch 1, 3 hdc in same sp, ★ 2 hdc in each ch-2 sp across to next corner ch-3 sp, (3 hdc, ch 1, 3 hdc) in corner sp; repeat from ★ 2 times **more**, 2 hdc in each ch-2 sp across, 2 hdc in same corner sp as first hdc; join with slip st to first hdc, finish off leaving a long end for sewing: 96 hdc and 4 corner ch-1 sps.

PLACEMENT DIAGRAM

C	B	B	A	A	B
B	B	A	A	B	B
B	A	A	B	B	C
A	A	B	B	C	C
A	B	B	C	C	B
B	B	C	C	B	B
B	C	C	B	B	A
C	C	B	B	A	A

ASSEMBLY

With **wrong** sides together, using Placement Diagram as a guide and working through **both** loops on **both** pieces, whipstitch Squares together with MC *(Fig. 5a, page 31)*, forming 6 vertical strips of 8 Squares each, beginning and ending in corner ch; then whipstitch stirips together in same manner.

EDGING

Rnd 1: With **right** side facing and working in Back Loops Only *(Fig. 1, page 30)*, join MC with sc in any corner ch-1 sp; sc in same sp and in next 24 hdc, ★ (sc in next joining and in next 24 hdc) across to next corner ch-1 sp, 3 sc in corner sp, sc in next 24 hdc; repeat from ★ 2 times **more**, (sc in next joining and in next 24 hdc) across, sc in same corner sp as first sc; join with slip st to **both** loops of first sc: 708 sc.

Rnd 2: Ch 3, 2 dc in same st as joining, ★ dc in next sc and in each sc across to center sc of next corner 3-sc group, 3 dc in center sc; repeat from ★ 2 times **more**, dc in next sc and in each sc across; join with slip st to first dc: 716 dc.

Rnd 3: Ch 3, 3 dc in next corner dc, ★ dc in next dc and in each dc across to center dc of next corner 3-dc group, 3 dc in corner dc; repeat from ★ 2 times **more**, dc in next dc and in each dc across; join with slip st to first dc: 724 dc.

Rnd 4: Ch 4, skip next dc, (dc, ch 3, dc) in next corner dc, ch 1, ★ skip next dc, (dc in next dc, ch 1, skip next dc) across to center dc of next corner 3-dc group, (dc, ch 3, dc) in corner dc, ch 1; repeat from ★ 2 times **more**, skip next dc, (dc in next dc, ch 1, skip next dc) across; join with slip st to first dc, finish off: 366 dc and 366 sps.

Rnd 5: With **right** side facing, join Color A with slip st in any corner ch-3 sp; ch 1, work (Puff St, ch 3, Puff St) in same sp, ch 2, ★ (work Puff St in next ch-1 sp, ch 2) across to next corner ch-3 sp, work (Puff St, ch 3, Puff St) in corner sp, ch 2; repeat from ★ 2 times **more**, (work Puff St in next ch-1 sp, ch 2) across; join with slip st to top of first Puff St: 370 Puff Sts and 370 sps.

Rnd 6: Slip st in next corner ch-3 sp, ch 2 (**counts as first hdc**), 4 hdc in same sp, ★ 2 hdc in next ch-2 sp and in each ch-2 sp across to next corner ch-3 sp, 5 hdc in corner sp; repeat from ★ 2 times **more**, 2 hdc in next ch-2 sp and in each ch-2 sp across; join with slip st to first hdc, finish off.

Design by Jennine DeMoss.

Lacy Strips

●●○○ EASY +

Finished Size: 48½" x 63¼" (123 cm x 160.5 cm)

SHOPPING LIST

Yarn (Medium Weight)

[4 ounces, 203 yards
(113 grams, 186 meters) per skein]:

☐ 11 skeins

Crochet Hook

☐ Size I (5.5 mm)
   or size needed for gauge

Additional Supplies

☐ Yarn needle

GAUGE INFORMATION

Each Square = 1½" (3.75 cm)

Each Strip = 4¾" wide (12 cm)

Gauge Swatch: 3¼" wide x 8½" long
   (8.25 cm x 21.5 cm)

Make 3 Squares.

Work Border Rnd 1, page 16: 32 sps.

Finish off.

STITCH GUIDE

CLUSTER (uses next 3 dc)

★ YO, insert hook in **next** dc, YO and pull up a loop, YO and draw through 2 loops on hook; repeat from ★ 2 times **more**, YO and draw through all 4 loops on hook.

SINGLE CROCHET 2 TOGETHER (abbreviated sc2tog)

Pull up a loop in next dc on **same** Strip, skip next joining, pull up a loop in next dc on **next** Strip, YO and draw through all 3 loops on hook (**counts as one sc**).

STRIP (Make 10)

Square (Make 22)

Rnd 1 (Right side)**:** Ch 4, 2 dc in fourth ch from hook (**3 skipped chs count as first dc**), ch 3, (3 dc in same ch, ch 3) 3 times; join with slip st to first dc, finish off: 12 dc and 4 ch-3 sps.

Note: Loop a short piece of yarn around any stitch to mark Rnd 1 as **right** side.

Border

The first round is worked with the **right** side of each Square facing throughout.

Rnd 1: With **right** side facing, join yarn with slip st in any ch-3 sp on first Square; ch 6 (**counts as first dc plus ch 3**), dc in same sp, ★ ch 2, work Cluster, ch 2, (dc, ch 3, dc) in next ch-3 sp, ch 2, work Cluster, ch 2, [YO twice, insert hook in next ch-3 sp, YO and pull up a loop, (YO and draw through 2 loops on hook) twice, YO twice, insert hook in any ch-3 sp on **next** Square, YO and pull up a loop, (YO and draw through 2 loops on hook) twice, YO and draw through all 3 loops on hook (**first side Square joining made)**]; repeat from ★ across to last Square, ch 2, work Cluster, ch 2, [(dc, ch 3, dc) in next ch-3 sp, ch 2, work Cluster, ch 2] 3 times; working across opposite side of each Square, † YO twice, insert hook in next ch-3 sp on **same** Square (same one used for first side square joining), YO and pull up a loop, (YO and draw through 2 loops on hook) twice, YO twice, insert hook in ch-3 sp on **next** Square (same one used for first side square joining), YO and pull up a loop, (YO and draw through 2 loops on hook) twice, YO and draw through all 3 loops on hook (**second side Square joining made)**, ch 2, work Cluster, ch 2, (dc, ch 3, dc) in next ch-3 sp, ch 2, work Cluster, ch 2 †; repeat from † to † across; join with slip st to first dc: 88 Clusters and 222 sps.

Rnd 2: Ch 1, ♥ (sc, ch 3, sc) in next ch-3 sp, ch 1, sc in next ch-2 sp, ch 1, sc in next Cluster, ch 1, sc in next ch-2 sp, (ch 1, sc) twice in next ch-3 sp, place marker around last ch-1 made for st placement, ★ ch 1, dc in next dc, ch 2, YO twice, † insert hook in next Cluster, YO and pull up a loop, (YO and draw through 2 loops on hook) twice †, YO twice, skip next 2 ch-2 sps, repeat from † to † once, YO and draw through all 3 loops on hook, ch 2, dc in next dc, ch 1, sc in next ch-3 sp; repeat from ★ across to last Square, ch 1, sc in same sp, place marker around last ch-1 made for st placement, ch 1, sc in next ch-2 sp, ch 1, sc in next Cluster, ch 1, sc in next ch-2 sp, ch 1 ♥; repeat from ♥ to ♥ once; join with slip st to first sc: 190 sts and 190 sps.

Rnd 3: Ch 3 (**counts as first dc**), † (2 dc, ch 3, 2 dc) in next ch-3 sp, dc in next st, (dc in next ch-1 sp and in next st) 4 times, (dc, ch 1, dc) in marked sp, remove marker and place around ch-1 just made for assembly, work one dc in each st and in each ch-1 sp and 2 dc in each ch-2 sp across to next marker, (dc, ch 1, dc) in marked sp, remove marker and place around ch-1 just made for assembly †, dc in next st, (dc in next ch-1 sp and in next st) 4 times, repeat from † to † once, (dc in next st and in next ch-1 sp) 4 times; join with slip st to first dc, finish off: 474 dc and 6 sps.

ASSEMBLY

With **wrong** sides of long edges together and working through **both** loops on **both** pieces, whipstitch Strips together (*Fig. 5b, page 31*), beginning in first marked ch-1 sp and ending in next marked ch-1 sp; then whipstitch remaining strips together in same manner. Remove markers once Strips are joined EXCEPT the markers on outer edge of outer strips.

EDGING

Remove markers as stitches are worked.

Rnd 1: With **right** side of short edge facing, join yarn with sc in marked ch-1 sp (***see Joining With Sc, page 30***); † ch 1, (sc in next dc, ch 1, skip next dc) 6 times, (sc, ch 2, sc) in next ch-3 sp, [ch 1, skip next dc, (sc in next dc, ch 1, skip next dc) 5 times, sc2tog, ch 1, skip next dc, (sc in next dc, ch 1, skip next dc) 5 times, (sc, ch 2, sc) in next ch-3 sp] 9 times, ch 1, (skip next dc, sc in next dc, ch 1) 6 times, sc in next marked ch-1 sp, ch 1, sc in next dc, ch 1 †, (skip next dc, sc in next dc, ch 1) across to next marked ch-1 sp, sc in marked sp, repeat from † to † once, (skip next dc, sc in next dc, ch 1) across; join with slip st to first sc.

Rnd 2: (Slip st in next ch-1 sp, ch 1) 7 times, † (slip st, ch 2, slip st) in next ch-2 sp, ch 1, [(slip st in next ch-1 sp, ch 1) 5 times, pull up a loop in next ch-1 sp (2 loops on hook), pull up a loop in next ch-1 sp and draw loop through both loops on hook, ch 1, (slip st in next ch-1 sp, ch 1) 5 times, (slip st, ch 2, slip st) in next ch-2 sp, ch 1] 9 times †, (slip st in next ch-1 sp, ch 1) across to next ch-2 sp, repeat from † to † once, (slip st in next ch-1 sp, ch 1) across; join with slip st to first slip st, finish off.

Design by Anne Halliday.

Shadow Boxes

●●○○ **EASY**

Finished Size: 48½" x 60½" (123 cm x 153.5 cm)

SHOPPING LIST

Yarn (Medium Weight)
[3.5 ounces, 170 yards
(100 grams, 156 meters) per skein]:

- ☐ MC (Beige) - 15 skeins
- ☐ Color A (Mustard) - 2 skeins
- ☐ Color B (Olive) - 2 skeins
- ☐ Color C (Rust) - 2 skeins

Crochet Hook
- ☐ Size J (6 mm)

  or size needed for gauge

Additional Supplies
- ☐ Yarn needle

GAUGE INFORMATION

One Motif = 6" (15.25 cm) square
Gauge Swatch: 3⅛" (8 cm) square
Work same as Motif thru Rnd 3: 40 dc
and 4 corner ch-2 sps.

STITCH GUIDE

FRONT POST TREBLE CROCHET *(abbreviated FPtr)*
YO twice, insert hook from **front** to **back** around post of dc indicated *(Fig. 3, page 31)*, YO and pull up a loop (4 loops on hook), (YO and draw through 2 loops on hook) 3 times.

MOTIF (Make 80 total)

Make the following number of motifs using the color indicated for Rnds 4 and 5: 26 with Color C and 27 **each** with Color A and Color B.

With MC, ch 5; join with slip st to form a ring.

Rnd 1 (Right side)**:** Ch 3 (**counts as first dc, now and throughout**), 15 dc in ring; join with slip st to first dc: 16 dc.

Note: Loop a short piece of yarn around any stitch to mark Rnd 1 as **right** side.

Rnd 2: Ch 1, sc in same st as joining and in next 3 dc, ch 3, (sc in next 4 dc, ch 3) around; join with slip st to first sc: 16 sc and 4 corner ch-3 sps.

Rnd 3: Ch 3, dc in next 3 sc, (3 dc, ch 2, 3 dc) in next corner ch-3 sp, ★ dc in next 4 sc, (3 dc, ch 2, 3 dc) in next corner ch-3 sp; repeat from ★ 2 times **more**; join with slip st to first dc, finish off: 40 dc and 4 corner ch-2 sps.

Rnd 4: With **right** side facing, join color indicated with sc in same st as joining *(see Joining With Sc, page 30)*; ★ sc in each dc across to next corner ch-2 sp, (sc, ch 2, sc) in corner sp; repeat from ★ 3 times **more**, sc in each dc across; join with slip st to first sc: 48 sc and 4 corner ch-2 sps.

Rnd 5: Ch 1, sc in same st as joining and in each sc across to next corner ch-2 sp, (sc, ch 2, sc) in corner sp, ★ sc in each sc across to next corner ch-2 sp, (sc, ch 2, sc) in corner sp; repeat from ★ 2 times **more**, sc in each sc across; join with slip st to first sc, finish off: 56 sc and 4 corner ch-2 sps.

Rnd 6: With **right** side facing, join MC with sc in any corner ch-2 sp; ch 2, sc in same sp and in next 2 sc, ★ † work FPtr around each of first 2 dc after corner sp on Rnd 3, skip next 2 sc from last sc made, sc in next 2 sc, [skip next 2 dc on Rnd 3, work FPtr around each of next 2 dc, skip next 2 sc from last sc made, sc in next 2 sc] twice †, (sc, ch 2, sc) in next corner ch-2 sp, sc in next 2 sc; repeat from ★ 2 times **more**, then repeat from † to † once; join with slip st to first sc: 64 sts and 4 corner ch-2 sps.

Rnd 7: (Slip st, ch 5, dc) in next corner ch-2 sp, ★ dc in next sc and in each st across to next corner ch-2 sp, (dc, ch 2, dc) in corner sp; repeat from ★ 2 times **more**, dc in next sc and in each st across; join with slip st to third ch of beginning ch-5: 72 sts and 4 corner ch-2 sps.

Rnd 8: (Slip st, ch 1, sc, ch 2, sc) in next corner ch-2 sp, ★ sc in each dc across to next corner ch-2 sp, (sc, ch 2, sc) in corner sp; repeat from ★ 2 times **more**, sc in each dc across; join with slip st to first sc, finish off leaving a long end for sewing: 80 sc and 4 corner ch-2 sps.

PLACEMENT DIAGRAM

A	B	C	A	B	C	A	B
B	C	A	B	C	A	B	C
C	A	B	C	A	B	C	A
A	B	C	A	B	C	A	B
B	C	A	B	C	A	B	C
C	A	B	C	A	B	C	A
A	B	C	A	B	C	A	B
B	C	A	B	C	A	B	C
C	A	B	C	A	B	C	A
A	B	C	A	B	C	A	B

ASSEMBLY

With **wrong** sides together, using Placement Diagram as a guide and working through **inside** loops on **both** pieces, whipstitch Squares together with MC *(Fig. 5c, page 31)*, forming 8 vertical strips of 10 Squares each, beginning in second ch of first corner and ending in first ch of next corner; then whipstitch strips together in same manner.

EDGING

With **right** side facing, join MC with sc in any corner ch-2 sp; ch 2, sc in same corner sp, sc in each sc around working (sc, ch 2, sc) in each corner ch-2 sp; join with slip st to first sc, finish off.

Design by Eleanor Albano-Miles.

Pebbled Pathway

●●○○ **EASY**

Finished Size: 49½" x 66½" (125.5 cm x 169 cm)

SHOPPING LIST

Yarn (Medium Weight)

[5 ounces, 256 yards
(141 grams, 234 meters) per skein]:
☐ MC (Spearmint) - 9 skeins
[4 ounces, 204 yards
(113 grams, 187 meters) per skein]:
☐ CC (Variegated) - 6 skeins

Crochet Hook

☐ Size I (5.5 mm)
   or size needed for gauge

Additional Supplies

☐ Yarn needle

GAUGE INFORMATION

One Strip = 3" wide x 66" long (7.5 cm x 167.5 cm)
Gauge Swatch: 2¼" x 8¼" (5.75 cm x 21 cm)
With MC, ch 27.
Work same as Strip thru Rnd 2: 72 sts.

STITCH GUIDE

TREBLE CROCHET (abbreviated tr)
YO twice, insert hook in st indicated, YO and pull up a loop (4 loops on hook),
(YO and draw through 2 loops on hook) 3 times.

FRONT POST TREBLE CROCHET (abbreviated FPtr)
YO twice, insert hook from **front** to **back** around post of dc indicated (*Fig. 3, page 31*), YO and pull up a loop (4 loops on hook), (YO and draw through 2 loops on hook) 3 times.

STRIP (Make 16)

With MC, ch 235.

Foundation Row (Right side)**:** Dc in fifth ch from hook **(4 skipped chs count as first tr)** and in each ch across to last ch, tr in last ch: 232 sts.

Note: Loop a short piece of yarn around any stitch to mark Foundation Row as **right** side.

Rnd 1: Ch 3 **(counts as first dc)**, do **not** turn; work 6 dc around last tr made; dc in free loop of each ch at base of each dc across **(Fig. 2, page 30)**; 7 dc around last tr, dc in each dc across; join with slip st to first dc, finish off: 474 dc.

Rnd 2: With **right** side facing, join CC with sc in same st as joining **(see Joining Sc, page 30)**; sc in same st, 2 sc in each of next 6 dc, † sc in next 2 dc, skip next dc, work FPtr around dc one row **below** next dc (fourth dc on Foundation Rnd), working in **front** of FPtr just made, work FPtr around dc one row **below** skipped dc (third dc on Foundation Rnd), skip next 2 dc from last sc made, sc in next 2 dc, ★ skip next 3 dc on Foundation Rnd, work FPtr around next dc, working in **front** of FPtr just made, work FPtr around third skipped dc, skip next 2 dc from last sc made, sc in next 2 dc; repeat from ★ across † to next 7-dc group, 2 sc in each of next 7 dc, repeat from † to † once; join with slip st to first sc, finish off: 488 sts.

Rnd 3: With **right** side facing and working in Back Loops Only **(Fig. 1, page 30)**, join MC with sc in same st as joining, † place marker around last sc made for joining, sc in next 13 sts, place marker around last sc made for joining †, sc in next 231 sts, repeat from † to † once, sc in each st across; join with slip st to **both** loops of first sc, finish off.

ASSEMBLY

With **wrong** sides of long edges together and working through **inside** loops on **both** pieces, whipstitch Strips together with MC **(Fig. 5d, page 31)**, beginning in first marked sc and ending in second marked sc; then whipstitch remaining strips together in same manner.

EDGING

With **right** side facing and working in Back Loops Only, join MC with sc in any sc; sc around entire afghan increasing and decreasing as necessary to keep piece lying flat; join with slip st to **both** loops of first sc, finish off.

Design by Jan Hatfield.

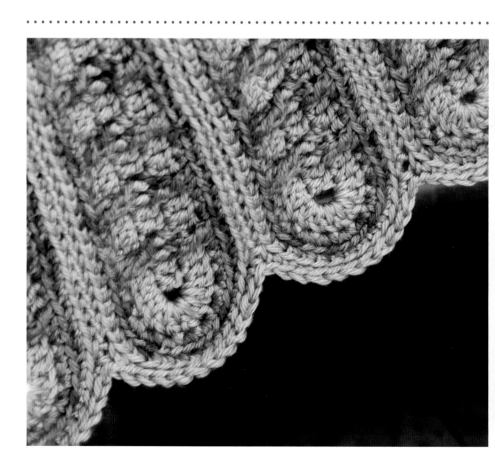

True Blue

 **EASY**

Finished Size: 44" x 58¼" (112 cm x 148 cm)

SHOPPING LIST

Yarn (Medium Weight)

[3.5 ounces, 246 yards
(100 grams, 225 meters) per skein]:

☐ MC (Blue) - 6 skeins

☐ CC (Grey) - 6 skeins

Crochet Hook

☐ Size I (5.5 mm)

or size needed for gauge

Additional Supplies

☐ Yarn needle

GAUGE INFORMATION

One Strip = 4" wide x 58¼" long
(10 cm x 148 cm)

6 rows = 4" (10 cm)

Gauge Swatch: 2³/₈" wide x 5¾" long
(6 cm x 14.5 cm)

Work same as Center through Row 6:
10 dc and one ch-2 sp.

STITCH GUIDE

TREBLE CROCHET *(abbreviated tr)*

YO twice, insert hook from **front** to **back** between 2 edge dc on **same** row, then from **back** to **front** between 2 edge dc on **next** row, YO and pull up a loop (4 loops on hook), (YO and draw through 2 loops on hook) 3 times.

FRONT POST TREBLE CROCHET *(abbreviated FPtr)*

YO twice, insert hook from **front** to **back** around post of st indicated *(Fig. 3, page 31)*, YO and pull up a loop (4 loops on hook), (YO and draw through 2 loops on hook) 3 times.

STRIP (Make 11)

Center (Make 6 with CC & 5 with MC)

Foundation Row (Right side)**:** With color indicated, ch 11, dc in fourth ch from hook **(3 skipped chs count as first dc)**, skip next 2 chs, (3 dc, ch 2, 3 dc) in next ch, skip next 2 chs, dc in next ch, ch 2, slip st in last ch **(first half made)**; ch 3 **(counts as first dc)**, working in free loops of beginning ch *(Fig. 2, page 30)*, dc in next ch, skip next 2 chs, (3 dc, ch 2, 3 dc) in next ch, skip next 2 chs, dc in next 2 chs **(second half made)**.

Note: Loop a short piece of yarn around any stitch to mark Foundation Row as **right** side **and** bottom edge.

Row 1: Ch 3 **(counts as first dc, now and throughout)**, turn; dc in next dc, (3 dc, ch 2, 3 dc) in next ch-2 sp, skip next 3 dc, dc in next dc and in next ch: 10 dc and one ch-2 sp.

Rows 2-82: Ch 3, turn; dc in next dc, (3 dc, ch 2, 3 dc) in next ch-2 sp, skip next 3 dc, dc in last 2 dc.

Finish off.

Border (Use MC on CC Center & use CC on MC Center)

Rnd 1: With **right** side facing and color indicated, join yarn with dc around post of dc at end of Row 82 *(see Joining With Dc, page 30)*; dc around same dc, work tr, place marker around tr just made for st placement, (2 dc around post of next dc, work tr) across to last ch-2 on first half of Foundation Row, place marker around last tr made for st placement, 2 dc around ch-2, work FPtr around next dc, dc in next 3 dc, 3 dc in next ch-2 sp, dc in next 3 dc, work FPtr around next dc, 2 dc around post of last dc on first half, work tr, place marker around tr just made for st placement, (2 dc around post of next dc, work tr) across to Row 82, place marker around last tr made for st placement, 2 dc around post of first dc on Row 82, work FPtr around next dc, dc in next 3 dc, 3 dc in next ch-2 sp, dc in next 3 dc, work FPtr around next dc; join with slip st to first dc.

Rnd 2: Ch 1, working in Back Loops Only *(Fig. 1, page 30)*, sc in same st as joining and in next 2 sts, † remove marker from marked st and place around last sc made for assembly, sc in each st across ending in next marked st, remove marker from marked st and place around last sc made for assembly, sc in next 7 sts, 4 sc in next dc †, sc in next 8 sts, repeat from † to † once, sc in last 5 sts; join with slip st to both loops of first sc, finish off.

ASSEMBLY

Beginning with Strip having MC Border, alternate Strips by Border color, ending with Strip having MC Border. Join Strips as follows:
With **wrong** sides of long edges together and working through **inside** loops on **both** pieces, whipstitch Strips together with MC *(Fig. 5d, page 31)*, beginning in first marked sc and ending in next marked sc; then whipstitch remaining strips together in same manner.

Design by Jan Hatfield.

General Instructions

ABBREVIATIONS

CC	Contrasting Color
ch(s)	chain(s)
cm	centimeters
dc	double crochet(s)
FPtr	Front Post treble crochet(s)
hdc	half double crochet(s)
MC	Main Color
mm	millimeters
Rnd(s)	Round(s)
sc	single crochet(s)
sc2tog	single crochet 2 together
sp(s)	space(s)
st(s)	stitch(es)
tr	treble crochet(s)
YO	yarn over

SYMBOLS & TERMS

★ — work instructions following ★ as many **more** times as indicated in addition to the first time.

† to † **or** ♥ to ♥ — work all instructions from first † to second † **or** from first ♥ to second ♥ **as many** times as specified.

( ) or [ ] — work enclosed instructions **as many** times as specified by the number immediately following **or** work all enclosed instructions in the stitch or space indicated **or** contains explanatory remarks.

colon (:) — the number(s) given after a colon at the end of a row or round denote(s) the number of stitches or spaces you should have on that row or round.

CROCHET TERMINOLOGY		
UNITED STATES		INTERNATIONAL
slip stitch (slip st)	=	single crochet (sc)
single crochet (sc)	=	double crochet (dc)
half double crochet (hdc)	=	half treble crochet (htr)
double crochet (dc)	=	treble crochet (tr)
treble crochet (tr)	=	double treble crochet (dtr)
double treble crochet (dtr)	=	triple treble crochet (ttr)
triple treble crochet (tr tr)	=	quadruple treble crochet (qtr)
skip	=	miss

Yarn Weight Symbol & Names	LACE 0	SUPER FINE 1	FINE 2	LIGHT 3	MEDIUM 4	BULKY 5	SUPER BULKY 6	JUMBO 7
Type of Yarns in Category	Fingering, size 10 crochet thread	Sock, Fingering, Baby	Sport, Baby	DK, Light Worsted	Worsted, Afghan, Aran	Chunky, Craft, Rug	Super Bulky, Roving	Jumbo, Roving
Crochet Gauge* Ranges in Single Crochet to 4" (10 cm)	32-42 sts**	21-32 sts	16-20 sts	12-17 sts	11-14 sts	8-11 sts	6-9 sts	5 sts and fewer
Advised Hook Size Range	Steel*** 6 to 8, Regular hook B-1	B-1 to E-4	E-4 to 7	7 to I-9	I-9 to K-10½	K-10½ to M/N-13	M/N-13 to Q	Q and larger

*GUIDELINES ONLY: The chart above reflects the most commonly used gauges and hook sizes for specific yarn categories.

** Lace weight yarns are usually crocheted with larger hooks to create lacy openwork patterns. Accordingly, a gauge range is difficult to determine. Always follow the gauge stated in your pattern.

*** Steel crochet hooks are sized differently from regular hooks–the higher the number, the smaller the hook, which is the reverse of regular hook sizing.

GAUGE

Exact gauge is **essential** for proper size. Before beginning your project, make the sample swatch given in the individual instructions in the yarn and hook specified. After completing the swatch, measure it, counting your stitches and rows/rounds carefully. If your swatch is larger or smaller than specified, **make another, changing hook size to get the correct gauge**. Keep trying until you find the size hook that will give you the specified gauge.

JOINING WITH SC

When instructed to join with a sc, begin with a slip knot on the hook. Insert hook in stitch or space indicated, YO and pull up a loop, YO and draw through both loops on hook.

JOINING WITH HDC

When instructed to join with a hdc, begin with a slip knot on the hook. YO, holding loop on hook, insert hook in stitch or space indicated, YO and pull up a loop, YO and draw through all 3 loops on hook.

JOINING WITH DC

When instructed to join with a dc, begin with a slip knot on the hook. YO, holding loop on hook, insert hook in stitch or space indicated, YO and pull up a loop (3 loops on hook), (YO and draw through 2 loops on hook) twice.

BACK LOOPS ONLY

Work only in loop(s) indicated by arrow *(Fig. 1)*.

Fig. 1

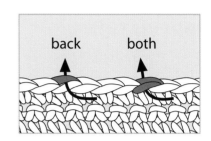

FREE LOOPS OF A CHAIN

When instructed to work in free loops of a chain, work in loop indicated by arrow *(Fig. 2)*.

Fig. 2

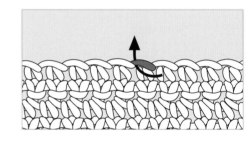

CROCHET HOOKS																
U.S.	B-1	C-2	D-3	E-4	F-5	G-6	7	H-8	I-9	J-10	K-10½	L-11	M/N-13	N/P-15	P/Q	Q	S
Metric - mm	2.25	2.75	3.25	3.5	3.75	4	4.5	5	5.5	6	6.5	8	9	10	15	16	19

POST STITCH

Work around post of stitch indicated, inserting hook in direction of arrow *(Fig. 3)*.

Fig. 3

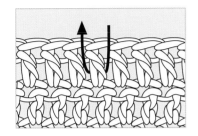

WORKING IN SPACE BEFORE A STITCH

When instructed to work in space **before** a stitch or in spaces **between** stitches, insert hook in space indicated by arrow *(Fig. 4)*.

Fig. 4

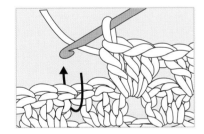

WHIPSTITCH

Place two Squares, Motifs, or Strips with **wrong** sides together. Sew through both pieces once to secure the beginning of the seam, leaving an ample yarn end to weave in later. Insert the needle from **front** to **back** through **both** loops on **both** pieces *(Figs. 5a & b)* **or** through **inside** loops only of each stitch on **both** pieces *(Figs. 5c & d)*. Bring the needle around and insert it from **front** to **back** through next loops of both pieces. Continue in this manner across, keeping the sewing yarn fairly loose.

Fig. 5a

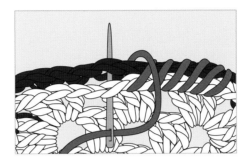

Fig. 5b

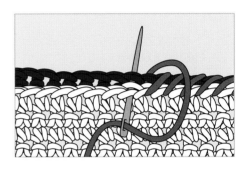

Fig. 5c

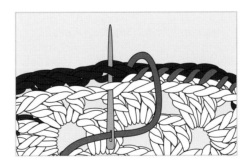

Fig. 5d

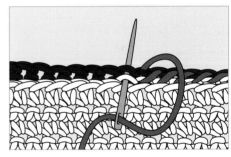

●○○○ BEGINNER	Projects for first-time crocheters using basic stitches. Minimal shaping.
●●○○ EASY	Projects using yarn with basic stitches, repetitive stitch patterns, simple color changes, and simple shaping and finishing.
●●●○ INTERMEDIATE	Projects using a variety of techniques, such as basic lace patterns or color patterns, mid-level shaping and finishing.
●●●● EXPERIENCED	Projects with intricate stitch patterns, techniques and dimension, such as non-repeating patterns, multi-color techniques, fine threads, small hooks, detailed shaping and refined finishing.

Yarn Information

Each Afghan in this book was made using Medium Weight Yarn. Any brand of Medium Weight Yarn may be used. It is best to refer to the yardage/meters when determining how many balls or skeins to purchase. Remember, to arrive at the finished size, it is the GAUGE/TENSION that is important, not the brand of yarn.

For your convenience, listed below are the specific yarns used to create our photography models. Because yarn manufacturers make frequent changes to their product lines, you may sometimes find it necessary to use a substitute yarn or to search for the discontinued product at alternate suppliers (locally or online).

AIRY SQUARES
Lion Brand® New Basic 175
MC - #113 Tomato
CC - #126 Espresso

SIMPLY PRETTY
Lion Brand® New Basic 175
MC - #150 Grey
Color A - #101 Peony
Color B - #149 Whisper

ALL-AROUND FAVORITE
Patons® Decor™
MC - #87614 Winter White
Color A - #87622 Rich Country Blue
Color B - #87621 Country Blue
Color C - #87620 Pale Country Blue

LACY STRIPS
Premier® Yarns Deborah Norville Collection™, Everyday®
#100-28 Mustard

SHADOW BOXES
Lion Brand® Vanna's Choice®
MC - #123 Beige
Color A - #158 Mustard
Color B - #174 Olive
Color C - #135 Rust

PEBBLED PATHWAY
Red Heart® Soft®
MC - #9623 Spearmint
CC - #9941 Watercolors

TRUE BLUE
Lion Brand® Jeans®
MC - #109W Stonewash
CC - #150Y Vintage

We have made every effort to ensure that these instructions are accurate and complete. We cannot, however, be responsible for human error, typographical mistakes, or variations in individual work.

Production Team: Instructional/Technical Editor - Linda A. Daley; Editorial Writer - Susan Frantz Wiles; Senior Graphic Artist - Lora Puls; Graphic Artist - Kellie McAnulty; Photo Stylist - Lori Wenger; and Photographer - Jason Masters.

Instructions tested and photo models made by Kimberly Holloway, Amanda Loggins, and Barbara Schou.